Feeling Down

The Way Back Up

by
**Roxane Brown Kunz
and Judy Harris Swenson**

Illustrated by
Mary McKee

DILLON PRESS, INC.
MINNEAPOLIS, MINNESOTA 55415

Library of Congress Cataloging in Publication Data

Kunz, Roxane Brown.
  Feeling down.

  (Understanding pressure)
  Summary: Explores the motives for a teenage girl's attempted
suicide and its effect on her brother and other family members.
    1. Suicide—Psychological   aspects—Juvenile   literature.
2. Youth—Suicidal behavior—Juvenile literature.   3. Suicide
victims—Family relationships—Juvenile literature.   4. Family
psychotherapy—Juvenile literature.   [1. Suicide]   I. Swenson, Judy Harris.   II. Title.   III. Series.
RJ506.S9K86   1986   616.85'8445   85-24604
ISBN 0-87518-326-3

Dillon Press, Inc., 242 Portland Avenue South
Minneapolis, Minnesota 55415

Printed in the United States of America
1 2 3 4 5 6 7 8 9 10 95 94 93 92 91 90 89 88 87 86

Foreword

Suicide is a sensitive subject. It is difficult to think, let alone talk, about it—especially when someone in the family has attempted suicide. The suicide or attempted suicide of a child arouses many feelings among parents, siblings, and friends. Anger, fear, and guilt are chief among the emotions that can confuse family members in the aftermath. "Why did it happen?" "Did I cause it?" "I wish she had really killed herself." "Is he mentally ill?" "Will she try it again?" These are some of the thoughts, often unspoken, that may run through their minds.

Judy Swenson and Roxanne Kunz have provided a very useful book for members of a family (especially siblings) in which one child has attempted suicide. They describe the experience through the eyes of a boy whose older sister, Stephanie, has recently tried to take her own life. The authors sensitively portray his feelings as he deals with this troubling event, including the family's involvement in psychotherapy.

Feeling Down: The Way Back Up not only talks about the family's reaction to Stephanie's attempt; it also shows what needs to be done to help the whole family. Swenson and Kunz urge more effective communication between family members but rightly add that communication is not enough; individuals in a family must also learn to cope more effectively with the stresses of life. The final pages of the book give specific suggestions for activities that can help alleviate the pressures on both "Stephanie" and other family members. In addition, their "Ideas for Discussion" can be used by the reader's family to encourage a greater flow of ideas and feelings among them.

The thought cannot be stressed enough: the problem of suicide is not just "Stephanie's"; it is also the family's. The support of each individual is needed for each other member of a family. It is difficult enough being human in this day and age; if the family becomes a place that *increases* the pressures we feel, then suicide, alcoholism, drug abuse, and the like will increase. If the family becomes a place of nurture (a tricky thing to achieve), then it can help to trim the pressures of living and prepare each member, child and adult, to re-enter the world outside. A nurturing family can serve as the foundation of one's sanity in a sometimes insane world.

—Howard Stone, Ph.D.
Brite Divinity School
Texas Christian University

Dr. Stone is the author of Crisis Counseling *(Philadelphia: Fortress Press, 1976) and* Suicide and Grief *(Philadelphia:Fortress Press, o.p.)*

Feeling Down

The Way Back Up

I woke when I heard Mom yelling my name. "Kirk, wake up. We need your help. Hurry!" My baby brother Sam was crying, and Mom wanted me to take care of him.

Our home was in total confusion. Dad was on the phone. I heard him say, "This is Jim Burton. Please send an ambulance to 210 Watkins Street."

Something was wrong with my teenage sister, Stephanie. Mom wouldn't let me in her room, but I could see her. She was very still, and her skin was chalk white. Mom called her name, but Stephanie didn't answer.

I was very scared. I didn't understand what

was happening. Finally, the ambulance came and took Stephanie to the hospital. Mom and Dad went with her. Our neighbor came to stay with Sam and me.

I had a hard time getting any sleep that night. When I woke up the next morning, Mom and Dad were home. They both looked tired and sad. Mom started to cry when Dad told me about Stephanie. Dad explained that Stephanie had almost died, and it wasn't because she had a disease. Her hurt and pain came from inside—her **feelings**. She wanted to run away from her problems. Stephanie had tried to kill herself. She had tried to commit **suicide**.

I jumped up and yelled, "Suicide, no way! Stephanie wouldn't do a thing like that." I ran to my room, slammed the door, and threw myself on the bed. My heart was pounding.

Before long, I heard my door squeak. Mom came in and sat down on my bed and put her arms around me. She spoke softly.

"I know what Stephanie tried to do is hard for you to understand. Dad and I don't understand, either. But what is important for now is that Stephanie is alive. We all need to be patient and hang in there together.

"Stephanie will not be able to come home until she is ready. Her body will heal quickly, but healing Stephanie's feelings will take more time," she told me.

I was still confused about what had happened and needed time to think. Later, I bombarded Mom and Dad with questions. Mom was right. She and Dad seemed as confused as I was.

Finally, Mom shouted, "We don't *have* answers to all of your questions." Then she said more softly, "Stephanie's **behavior** is a mystery to us, Kirk. Someone outside our family, a **therapist**, is going to help. I guess there are things we all need to understand about our own feelings as well as Stephanie's."

I was nervous about seeing a therapist.

Talking to a stranger about my family didn't seem right. I wanted Mom or Dad to be in charge. When I told them this, they looked surprised.

Dad answered, "Kirk, this is the biggest problem our family has ever had. We need to do all that we can to help Stephanie. I just don't think we can do it alone."

The next day, Mom and Dad said that we had to go to the hospital. I didn't want to go, but I had no choice. After visiting Stephanie, the four of us met with the therapist. I was glad to find that the therapist wasn't scary at all. Her name was Terri, and she helped me feel comfortable.

After talking with us for a while, Terri said,

11

"Your family has some problems to work on before Stephanie can come home."

What a shocker! I didn't know our family had problems. I thought this was Stephanie's problem.

I began to feel **guilty**. Was it my fault that Stephanie had tried to hurt herself? We had had a big fight two days before it happened. I said some things to her that I didn't mean, and she told me to get out of her life.

Stephanie and I don't always get along, but I love her. She is important to me. I swallowed the lump I felt in my throat as I shared some of these thoughts and feelings with Terri and my family.

Terri listened to me and didn't interrupt. When I finished she said, "You are all good people. Being here tells me that you care. No one should be blamed for Stephanie's attempted suicide."

"But why did she do it?" Mom asked, looking at Stephanie. Stephanie just kept staring at the floor.

Terri said that there were many reasons for Stephanie's behavior, and learning to **communicate** better would help us understand. She explained that communicating means talking honestly about feelings that are important to us.

"I know how to communicate," I said. "Didn't I just tell you what was on my mind?"

Terri smiled and said, "Communicating is only the first part of what you all need to learn. You also need to learn new ways to **cope** with **pressure**."

I didn't understand what Terri was talking about. *Cope* and *pressure* were new words for me, so I asked what they were.

Terri explained, "Cope is how you handle a problem. Pressure is what you feel when there is too much to handle. Having too much pressure to cope with can be a **burden**."

Dad sat up really straight in his chair, crossed his arms, and his face turned red. He looked like he was ready to explode. His voice boomed.

"What do you mean by burdens and pressures? Stephanie doesn't have it any harder than the rest of us. She's the oldest, so she *should* do more."

Terri didn't act upset with Dad. She said, "I understand how you feel. Everyone in a family has to help."

All of a sudden Stephanie started to cry. She said, "All I ever do is help, and it's never good enough. No one will let me be myself. There is no time for me."

Terri turned to Stephanie and said, "Let's talk about what is expected of you. Why don't we make a list?"

Terri made a list on the chalkboard of the things Stephanie said were expected of her.

1. Straight A's in school
2. Chores at home
3. Babysit for Sam on Saturdays
4. Help Kirk with paper route and homework
5. Clean house for Grandma
6. Practice piano 45 minutes every day
7. Act and look like a young lady

I looked at that list and thought, Wow, what a list. I started to feel sorry for Stephanie. I was glad I didn't have to do that much.

Terri turned to Mom and Dad and said, "Do you think that too much is expected of Stephanie?" Mom and Dad didn't answer. Then Terri turned to Stephanie. "When you were unable to cope with all of the pressure, you looked for an escape. What were your reasons for choosing suicide?"

Stephanie's face looked so sad when she answered. "I thought that it was an easy way out. I didn't know what else to do. I couldn't handle my problems."

Everyone was quiet for a while. Mom was the first to speak. "You know, Terri, it seems that everyone in our family, except the baby, is under pressure. Jim travels in his job. He's gone from home a lot, and I have to be in charge. I don't always have time to listen to the kids."

Terri nodded and said, "Let's talk about pressures. Will each of you share yours?"

Stephanie began. "Last year we moved, and I had to change schools. It was awful. I still don't have any friends. I want to please my parents and get top grades, but it's hopeless. I'm flunking at school. I hate my life."

When my turn came, I had to think really hard about my pressures. I told everyone, "It's easy for me to make new friends, and I like school. My biggest problem is my paper route.

My customers expect the papers delivered on time, and the boss gets angry with me if they complain to him. Trying to please my customers and boss all the time is impossible."

Next Dad spoke up. "Having a family is a big **responsibility**. I worry about making enough money to pay the bills."

Terri said, "Everyone has pressures in life. It seems as though Stephanie has a harder time than the rest of you. She needs more help adjusting to change and learning how to cope."

When we got home, I began to think about how our lives had changed. Because of Stephanie, we had to cancel a weekend camping trip. Dad said that taking care of her was costing a lot of money and taking a lot of time.

This didn't seem fair to me. Everyone seemed to be feeling sorry for Stephanie, but I didn't anymore. I thought she was acting like a big baby. Stephanie had hurt me, too, when she tried to commit suicide. She was selfish.

Besides that, all the kids at school talked about Stephanie. I was embarrassed. One day I heard Rick Ryan say, "Stephanie Burton must be a real psycho."

That did it. I slugged him and ended up in the office of the school principal, Mr. Holloway. I felt like everything was wrong in my world.

Was I surprised to discover that talking with Mr. Holloway made me feel better! He helped me understand that I had angry feelings about what had happened to Stephanie. We talked about other ways that I could handle my **anger**.

Mr. Holloway said, "Sharing your feelings with a friend sometimes helps." He also brought up the things kids were saying about Stephanie. "Kirk," he said, "the kids at school aren't trying to be mean. They are curious and uncomfortable about Stephanie's behavior. Sometimes people just don't know what to say."

I left Mr. Holloway's office feeling better. He had helped me to understand myself and the other kids. Now it would be easier to handle my problems at school.

The next week when we saw Terri, I talked about my fight at school and how I had behaved. When I finished, Terri used some new words to describe the way I acted. Terri called my fighting **inappropriate behavior**. If I had talked about my feelings with Rick, she said that I would have used **appropriate behavior**.

Terri said, "Kirk seems to be having a hard time in school right now. Stephanie, would you tell us how things are when you're in school?"

Stephanie looked sad. "Not the greatest," she answered. "I wish I could feel better about school.

Sometimes I ditch class. I know I shouldn't, but it's better than feeling like I don't belong."

"Stephanie," Terri said, "I know you have been in pain, but you can't run away from your problems. There are better ways to cope with the pain that you feel. Ditching class is inappropriate behavior. You have to learn to communicate and face things the way they are. This is **reality**."

Stephanie said, "It's hard to cope at home. Mom is too busy to listen, and she doesn't understand me. She is old fashioned and always says no. We can't agree on much of anything. Mom criticizes everything—my music, the magazines I read, the clothes I wear. Her way is the only way."

Stephanie went on and on. She complained, "Dad is gone so much, and when he is home, all he wants is peace and quiet. He takes Mom's side when there is trouble.

"Dad plays with my baby brother a lot, too. He and Mom laugh at everything that he does. It isn't fair how Sam gets all the attention."

As Stephanie talked, her voice got louder and louder. She was so angry that she began to shout. My head hurt. I plugged my ears.

When Stephanie stopped shouting, Terri looked at each of us and said, "This family is not communicating with each other. You need to rec- ognize your anger and express it in the right way. So far, shouting and ignoring each other haven't worked. These behaviors are a waste of time and make you tired. Let me help you practice talking and listening to each other."

In the next few weeks, Terri helped us to communicate better with each other. To begin, one person talked, and everyone listened. Then we took turns telling what each of us said. Repeating what we heard was hard because we had to use our own words. I really had to listen carefully.

Terri had another way for us to communicate with each other. "Write down your feelings if it is hard to talk about them," she suggested.

Writing helped us express our feelings of **stress**. We wrote down our bottled-up feelings and let them go. Our family called these our "let go letters." If we wanted to, we shared our letters with each other.

Everyone in our family was learning. It was slow, but things were getting better. Mom and Dad started to ask us how we felt about things. Stephanie and I began to say what was on our minds. We really had to work at listening to one another. Sometimes this was hard, especially when we were angry or sad. But, we kept trying.

A few weeks later, when our family met with Terri, Stephanie talked about communicating.

"Learning how to communicate takes practice," she said, "but it's worth it. Sharing my thoughts and feelings and listening to others help me understand other people better.

"Too bad I didn't know earlier how to communicate in a healthy way. I wanted to show you how rotten I felt. I cried a lot and dragged myself around the house. Finally, I just stayed in my room and slept. Nothing seemed to matter anymore. I even gave my favorite posters and my radio to Kirk."

"Stephanie, there's a word to explain how you acted," said Terri. "You were **withdrawn**. You stayed away from everyone. **Depressed** is the word that is used to describe how you felt. You were sad inside.

"Your body gave signals to everyone, but you didn't know it. When you frowned a lot, cried, slumped your shoulders, and dragged your feet, you were using **body language**. Body language is another way to communicate."

All of a sudden, Stephanie's attempted suicide began to make sense to me. Gosh, I thought, Stephanie's body had been trying to tell me that she was unhappy.

I remembered when I first noticed changes in Stephanie. After we moved, she hardly ate anything at dinner. I thought she looked skinny.

Stephanie said that her stomach hurt all the time. Mom took her to the doctor, but he couldn't find anything wrong. Looking back, I saw that body language was really important.

I remembered the night that Stephanie tried to kill herself. After dinner, I had heard crying in her room. I popped in to see what was wrong.

Stephanie hid her face in the pillow and mumbled, "Get out and leave me alone. Everything is hopeless. I have nothing to look forward to anymore."

I patted her on the back and left the room. Stephanie was so unhappy, and I couldn't do anything to help her. I felt bad. Later that night, Stephanie attempted suicide. Ever since then, our family has been learning to understand why Stephanie tried to end her life.

Terri summed it up by saying, "Stephanie sent out signals for help when she was not able to cope with pressures. Many times these signals act as a warning. These are the warning signs to know."

Possible Warning Signs for Suicide

1. Big change in sleeping habits
2. Body changes (health habits, weight gain or loss)
3. Giving one's belongings away

4. Big changes in behavior (withdrawn, angry, or a lot of inappropriate behavior)
5. Illness without any known physical cause
6. Unusual changes at school (grades, attendance, behavior)
7. Use of alcohol, drugs, or other substances harmful to the body
8. Too much interest in death
9. Talking about ending one's life or a past suicide attempt
10. Running away from home or school

Now, knowing the suicide signs might help me to help someone else.

After weeks of working with Terri, Stephanie told us that she was ready to come home. I was excited but a little **nervous**. I wondered how to act. Could I still joke and play tricks? I also worried that Stephanie might try suicide again. When we met with Terri, I told her my fears. Mom and Dad said that they were nervous, too.

Terri helped us all feel better when she said, "It's natural for you to feel this way, but you're ready to have Stephanie come home. Think of the changes you've made. You are communicating better, handling your anger in more appropriate ways, and changing what you expect from Stephanie.

"Stephanie is different, too. Now she is facing reality, coping better with pressure, and making some plans that will help her feel better about herself. It's time for this family to relax! Just be yourselves."

Our family is lucky to have someone like Terri to help us. The worst part is over, but we still have work to do. Stephanie's feelings will be healing for a long time. Our family will always need to work hard at communicating.

Now we know that we can work out and solve our problems. We are learning to understand our feelings and behaviors, to make better choices, and to cope when there is pressure and stress.

Glossary

anger—a strong feeling of unhappiness that is often out of control and hurtful to others

appropriate behavior—an acceptable way to act

behavior—how one acts

body language—to communicate by using one's body instead of words

burden—a responsibility that causes worry or pressure

communicate—to share information by speaking, writing, or body language

cope—how one handles a problem

depressed—feeling sad

feelings—strong emotions like sadness, joy, and anger

guilty—feeling responsible for something (usually wrong or harmful) that has happened

inappropriate behavior—an unacceptable way to act

nervous—feeling uneasy or unsure of one's self

pressure—what one feels when there is too much to handle

reality—the way something really is

responsibility—one's duty

stress—a feeling of pressure

suicide—to end one's life on purpose

therapist—a person trained to help people solve their problems

withdrawn—staying away from people, and not taking part in what is going on

Adult Resource Guide

The existence of suicide cannot be denied. It involves all age groups and can affect an entire community. This book has been written to aid those affected by suicide attempts and to encourage positive solutions for coping with overwhelming pressures.

Feeling Down: The Way Back Up is designed to educate and create an awareness of suicide. This, however, is not a suicide prevention book. Professional help should be sought for any emotional problems that seem overwhelming.

The following suggested activities and selected bibliography are offered for further education and to help children cope with the pressures of everyday life that can lead to the hopeless feelings that sometimes result in suicide.

Questions for Discussion

1. What pressures do you have in your life? How do you cope with them now?

2. How could you improve your coping skills?

3. What ways do you use to communicate with others?

4. Everyone feels down sometimes. This is normal. The important thing is how people cope with their feelings when they are down or depressed. Have you ever felt down or depressed? How did you feel? What was happening when you became depressed? What can you do to help yourself feel better when you are depressed? Who can you talk to when you feel down?

5. What kinds of things can you do to help others feel good? What kind of behavior can hurt others?

6. Do you know anyone who has tried to commit suicide? How did this make you feel?

7. How are other people affected when someone tries to commit suicide?

Activity Suggestions

A. Work through each of the ten possible warning signs for suicide.

1. Big change in sleeping habits
2. Body changes (health habits, weight gain or loss)
3. Giving one's belongings away
4. Big changes in behavior (withdrawn, angry, or a lot of inappropriate behavior)
5. Illness without any known physical cause
6. Unusual changes at school (grades, attendance, behavior)
7. Use of alcohol, drugs, or other substances harmful to the body
8. Too much interest in death
9. Talking about ending one's life or a past suicide attempt
10. Running away from home or school

(Clarify the meaning of each of the above signs, and explain that everyone may have some of these signs sometimes. Emphasize that no one is responsible for another person's behavior or the choices a person makes. Stimulate suggestions for what people can do to help if they notice any of these signs in someone.)

B. Stress Reduction Activities

1. Everyone has a bad day sometimes. Read *Alexander and the Terrible, Horrible, No Good, Very Bad Day* by Judith Viorst. What could Alexander have done to make his day better? How did Alexander cope with pressure?

2. Use body language to show anger, joy, sadness, excitement, and nervousness.

3. Art helps to express feelings. Fingerpainting, drawing with chalk or crayons, or working with clay or mud can be an effective release for tension.

4. Relaxing music can soothe a stressful mind. While playing soft music, have the child lie down, take deep breaths, close his/her eyes, and pretend to be at a favorite place.

5. Physical exercise is another way to handle stress. Exercise can include bicycling, dancing, swimming, running, basketball, and other sports. Simple exercises are also helpful.
   There are adaptations for handicapped children. Always be sure the child is healthy before beginning a new exercise program.

6. Play out new situations in "Let's Pretend!" Practice may help a child be ready to cope with pressure.
   a) You are a new kid at school. You don't know anyone and are very lonely. What will you do?
   b) You're having trouble with your school work. You know your parents will be angry. What do you do?
   c) You are angry with one of your friends. How will you behave?

C. Communication Builders

1. Work in pairs if you are dealing with more than one child. One child interviews the other to find out as much as possible about that person in one minute. Have the children switch places. The person being interviewed may refuse to answer any question with which he or she is uncomfortable. When finished, everyone shares with the group something they have learned about the person they interviewed.

2. An old-fashioned buzz game is a great way to improve listening skills. A group of children sit in a

circle. The first child whispers a word to the next child. The word is whispered from one child to another until it reaches the last person. The last person repeats the word. The first word often becomes very distorted. Next time around, the first person is last, and the second person is first.

3. Giving and receiving compliments help children feel good about themselves. In a small group, go around in a circle and let every child have a turn giving a compliment to each person. These must be sincere compliments and something other than physical appearance or academic ability. The child who receives the compliment should listen carefully and say thank you.

Resources

1. There are suicide hotlines and suicide prevention centers in many communities. Local hospitals may offer support services as well. Check your telephone book.

2. If your community has the emergency number 911, remember it and use it in a crisis situation. See that children know this number as well.

Selected Bibliography

Gordon, Sol. *When Living Hurts*. New York: Union of American Hebrew Congregations, 1985.

Griffin, Mary, M.D., and Carol Felsenthal. *A Cry for Help*. New York: Doubleday, 1983.

Kuczen, Barbara. *Childhood Stress: Don't Let Your Child Be a Victim*. New York: Delacorte Press, 1982.

Madison, Arnold. *Suicide and Young People*. New York: Clarion Books, 1981.

Saunders, Antoinette, and Bonnie Remsberg. *The Stress Proof Child*. New York: Holt, Rinehart & Winston, 1984.

Seiden, R.H. *Suicide Among Youth*. Washington, D.C.: U.S. Government Printing Office, 1969.

Stone, Howard. *Crisis Counseling*. Philadelphia: Fortress Press, 1976.

About the Authors

Roxane Kunz and Judy Swenson became acquainted in 1969 when they were third grade teachers at the same school. Both hold Masters degrees in education. Their common interest in education soon expanded into a close friendship with a variety of shared interests. They both love to be outside in their home state of Arizona.

Roxane works full-time as a school psychologist and is a certified reality therapist. Her expertise as a practicing professional blends well with Judy's full-time involvement as a professional volunteer in a variety of school and community programs. Judy is married and the mother of two active boys. Roxane is married and the mother of one grown son.

Judy and Roxane wrote *Feeling Down: The Way Back Up* because they saw a need for children to understand the everyday pressures that may lead to the hopeless feelings which often result in suicide, and to provide children and caring adults with coping and communication skills as possible solutions for dealing with overwhelming pressures.